GIVING
GOD'S DIVINE EXCHANGE RATE

Written By

Gregory & Teresa McCurry

Copyright © 2019 by Teresa S. McCurry
All rights reserved. This book or any portion thereof may not be reproduced or used in any manner whatsoever without the express written permission of the publisher except for the use of brief quotations in a book review.

Printed in the United States of America

First Printing, 2019

ISBN 978-1-7338770-1-5 (sc)
ISBN 978-1-7338770-4-6 (e)

McCurry Ministries International
2060 West 65th Street
Cleveland, Ohio 44102
(216) 916-9270

www.MyNewBeginning.org

FOREWORD

Giving is a characteristic of love: St. John 3:16 in the King James Version of the Bible declares that, "God so loved the world that He GAVE His only begotten Son, that whosoever believeth in him should not perish but have everlasting life."

God is love. We can show our love for God and mankind through our giving. The benefits of giving are so amazing. According to Luke 6:38, "Give and it shall be given back to you, good measure…" Men shall also give to you.

Apostle McCurry and Pastor Tee have been awesome examples of what they are teaching in this series: read, observe, and be tremendously blessed, and be determined to apply the teaching to your daily life, and watch as God blesses you abundantly. I have personally experienced the blessings from the word of God ministered by this power couple, Apostle Greg and my Spiritual Daughter & cousin, Pastor Tee. They have taken the time to share the truth from God's word about giving so that everyone who reads this book will have the opportunity to experience the goodness of God on a greater level. As we gain a better understanding on what the word of God says about giving.

Lovingly, Mom
Pastor Pamela Westbrook

FOREWORD II

I Corinthians 8:9 says, "That Jesus became poor so that you could be rich from the inside out."

My son is a wonderful example of this teaching. Now you have the honour of hearing his testimony and to join him in your own personal study and application of instruction so that, by the help of the Holy Spirit, you will learn how to receive and give like never before; and to become rich from the inside out.

You are going to enjoy this book on God's Exchange Rate for giving, Greg and Teresa live a life of abundance because they follow the principals in the book. Take this as a personal invitation from a new friend and receive your own testimony about how you got rich from the inside out.

Greg is one of my heroes and an inspiration to me. Now allow my son to become an inspiration to you too.

Love Dad.

Chief Apostle Leon D. Nelson, Jr.

ACKNOWLEDGEMENTS

"We have to start by thanking our Amazing Church family, New Beginning Ministries, you are the BEST that God can give. We are so honoured to be called your pastors, we love the fact that God called us to Shepherd each and every one of you. He called us to "Introduce a REAL God, to REAL People with REAL ISSUES", and we enjoy every minute of it. We love the Faith, Family & Fellowship that we get in this place.

I, Teresa, would be remised if I did not say thank you to "Christian Fellowship Centre Ministries, my church home for over 17 years. Most of the teachings on giving I learned from my Spiritual father, the Late Bishop Bill McKinney, from watching him on television every Sunday night before I joined to sitting under the powerful anointing on Sunday morning.

I am the giver that I am today because of his simple yet practical teaching. We have inserted some excerpts from his book, "GIVE THE MAN HIS DOUGH: How to receive a Ministry Gift", throughout this book in his loving Memory.

I, Greg, am so excited that God saw it fit to bring both of us givers together to be a blessing to the kingdom of God, and reap the harvest from the seeds that we sow on 7/7/07 @ 7 when Teresa and I said "I DO", a supernatural manifestation of God has truly taken place. To my Spiritual father chief- Apostle Leon Nelson, the ultimate GIVER, I cannot thank you enough for the imprint that you have left on my life – a mark that can never be erased. To our content editor Kenneth Ndlovu, this project would not be complete without your final edits, thank you. We decree and declare a hundred-fold blessing to you from every seed that you sow into the kingdom of God.

In his service

Apostle Gregory & Sr. Pastor Teresa McCurry

LIST OF IN-TEXT TESTIMONIALS

1. Margie Nelson...Page 11
2. Alvin & Helen Copeland................................Page 19
3. Nichelle N. Daniels, MIT..............................Page 30
4. Pstr. Denise Washington................................Page 31
5. Angela Hunter...Page 39
6. Yolanda D. Hamilton......................................Page 44
7. Elder Natasha Williams.................................Page 49
8. Ms. Delicia Mayes R.T. (R.) (MR)...............Page 56
9. Pstr. Adreane Russell......................................Page 69
10. Sis. Shanel Williams......................................Page 75
11. Sis. Shawnda Slaughter................................Page 76
12. Sis. Richanda Jackson..................................Page 78
13. Deacon Reginald Walker.............................Page 79

CONTENTS

Foreword iii

Foreword II v

Acknowledgements vi

List Of In-Text Testimonials viii

Introduction xi

Chapter One: God's Love - Foundation For Giving 1

Chapter Two: The Divine Exchange Rate 7

Chapter Three: Tithes 18

Chapter Four: Offerings 33

Chapter Five: First Fruit 45

Chapter Six: Alms 50

Chapter Seven: Other Ways Of Giving 57

Chapter Eight: Benefits Giving 61

Chapter Nine: Right Attitude For Profitable Giving .. 70

Chapter Ten: More Testimonials 74

Questions And Answers Section	80
About The Authors Apostle Gregory McCurry	82
Teresa (Pastor Tee) McCurry	84
Appendix 1: Resources Used	87

INTRODUCTION

Welcome to your season of unprecedented abundance. What a privilege it is to know God and His principles for life and prosperity. We don't deserve it, we cannot earn it; it is what it is- Grace and unmerited favour in the Lord Jesus Christ!

My friend, this promises to be an amazing experience. The book you are reading is filled with anointed, inspiring, insightful and even challenging words.

It will re-engineer your mind towards the concept of 'giving' and make you walk in financial overflow – all your needs will be met, and you will have plenty and more to put in store.

We write this being guided by the belief that God has His own way of working with numbers, this is no longer the US Federal Reserve's ways, nor is it coming from your trusted stock broker who tells you to spin a couple of thousands for a few percentage points gains in value, not at all.

This is God who says when you give, you will reap a hundredfold, a thousand-fold and so much more. This is the same God who says will give back pressed down, shaken together, in good measure and that where His blessings come from, there is a continued overflow, unlike your investor who gets affected by bad inflation and falling or rising commodity prices, depending on your investment position!

Redemption generates prosperity

We have put up the heading with two words in redemption and prosperity, and that the latter is as a direct result of the former. Therefore, it puts us to the direct evidence that being in Christ is something that revolves around processes, and before we delve much into the teachings in this book, you might want to know that these processes start far back, from as far as when you decide to become part of the family of Christ, when you get saved and eventually the part when you get baptised, completing the process that ushers you into the Kingdom of God.

All the above points to processes, and so is the process to prosperity, which starts at redemption stage. Having said that, it becomes quite imperative to also mention the fact that this process is not just like redemption equals prosperity, but there are also so many variables that come into this equation, which is the reason behind this book – to explain one of the important variables – Giving!

Firstly, we want to draw your attention to an overwhelmingly evident fact. This may sound familiar to you or even strange, yet we want you to receive it with a heart of openness and expectation. Remember that the key to fully understanding something is always to be expectant when the message is being conveyed.

We want to let you in on the fact that, redemption through Christ launches us into a prosperous, wealthy, rich and abundant life. Oh my! This is so true and clear throughout the scriptures! Join us as we bring you into a fresh reality of this liberating truth.

The truth is, Jesus did not die for us to just live from hand to mouth. We were not saved to be poor or to live on scrap. We were not destined to be pitied, but we were called to Glory and Grace. This all should be experienced right in front of everyone so that the world knows that we serve God who is bale to exceedingly look after His own people.

Speaking of being blessed right in front of people and the art of giving, do you know that you could be giving in secrecy, just helping out at the local school with anonymous hampers, anonymous cheques and so forth, and when God blesses you for your work, He will do it in public so that the world knows how good He is to keeping His word. You should know that sowing is sowing when in the Kingdom of God, it does not matter whether you do it in public or in secrecy.

Anyways, we were not called to be slaves of men or live at the mercy of others, NO! We were called to be servants of a blessed and prosperous God. We were called not to beg and bow before men, or be men-worshippers so that we could eat of the crumbs from their table, NO! Ours is a portion from where happiness and abundancy are.

Psalm 35:27 (AMPC)

Let those who favor my righteous cause and have pleasure in my uprightness shout for joy and be glad and say continually, Let the Lord be magnified, Who takes pleasure in the prosperity of His servant.

God indeed takes pleasure, and is rightly delighted in the prosperity of His people. This is so because He has the means, and is so resourceful enough to bless all of His people. Our God is not broke! He said that silver and gold are mine, and the cattle on a thousand hills.

Psalm 50:10 (AMPC)

For every beast of the forest is Mine, and the cattle upon a thousand hills or upon the mountains where thousands are.

More so, our God is not only prosperous, but He also delights in the prosperity of His servants as mentioned before. The utmost desire of God for the redeemed, here on earth is clearly for His people to live a good life whilst on earth. This is rightly expressed in the following scripture which we hope for you to read slowly so that you get the deeper meaning that it is conveying.

3 John 2 (AMPC)

> *Beloved, I pray that you may prosper in every way and [that your body] may keep well, even as [I know] your soul keeps well and prospers.*

So, we are called to a prosperous life in our Spirit, Soul and Body, regardless of what level we may be today. It is important also to first agree with this promise of God in our minds regardless of the picture of our present reality, because in life, whatever is happening today, will definitely not determine where you end up tomorrow, but how you commit to life and God's principles and teachings does. Because as a man thinks in his heart so is he.

Proverbs 23:7 (AMPC)

> *For as he thinks in his heart, so is he. As one who reckons, he says to you, eat and drink, yet his heart is not with you [but is grudging the cost].*

Too much money is NOT a "spiritual risk"

Unfortunately, some people believe that prosperity is not, and cannot be associated with "Holiness", and when you are rich you are less likely to 'make it into' heaven. Likewise, some just want to go around the same cycle and remain there but the Heartbeat of God is that we **prosper in all things** and be in health just as your soul prospers (3 John 2).

Interestingly, the Bible says, *"And if ye be Christ's, then are ye Abraham's seed, and heirs according to the promise* (Gal 3:29), and in Genesis 12: 2 we see part of the promise; *"And I will make of thee a great nation, and I will bless thee, and make thy name great; and thou shalt be a blessing."*

According to the above, we are therefore the seeds of Abraham and heirs according to the promise. By implication, we have a heritage of not just becoming blessed but to be a blessing to people in our present age and even many generations to come.

Are you saved? If yes, then you have no business with poverty. Welcome to a life of ceaseless flow of God's provision. In fact, we challenge you to tell yourself at this point- "No more dry seasons." The reason why we want you to tell yourself this is the fact that there is power in declaration, where whatever you tell yourself that you are, is exactly what is likely to happen to you because the positive talk brews positive energy around you, and above all, it is a sign of great faith in God which ultimately brings you reaping the rewards of your faith in Him.

Jesus was "poor"; He is my role model...

Most people ignorantly desire poverty because they feel they will become more like Jesus by being poor than if they were rich. These people think Jesus was a 'poor' man when he was here on earth. They defend their ignorance with such verses as the one below:

2 Corinthians 8:9 (AMPC)

For you are becoming progressively acquainted with and recognizing more strongly and clearly the grace of our Lord Jesus Christ (His kindness, His gracious generosity, His undeserved favor and spiritual blessing), [in] that though He was [so very] rich, yet for your sakes He became [so very] poor, in order that by His poverty you might become enriched (abundantly supplied).

However, permit us to enlighten you more on how 'poor' Jesus was. It is amazing to realize that, 'POOR' Jesus travels with minimum twelve mature and responsible men (some were married with children); He had a personal accountant to handle His finances in person of Judas Iscariot; He had enough fund to travel with a boat (that has a private apartment for Him to sleep while on the sea)alongside His disciples, He had access to heaven's wealth so much that, that He wasn't owing tax, see the scripture below:

Matthew 17:24-27 (AMPC)

The Tribute Money

24 When they arrived in Capernaum, the

collectors of the half shekel [the temple tax] went up to Peter and said, Does not your Teacher pay the half shekel?

25 He answered, Yes. And when he came home, Jesus spoke to him [about it] first, saying, What do you think, Simon? From whom do earthly rulers collect duties or tribute—from their own sons or from others [k]not of their own family?

26 And when Peter said, From other people [l]not of their own family, Jesus said to him, Then the sons are exempt.

27 However, in order not to give offense and cause them to stumble [that is, to cause them [m]to judge unfavorably and unjustly] go down to the sea and throw in a hook. Take the first fish that comes up, and when you open its mouth you will find there a shekel. Take it and give it to them to pay the temple tax for Me and for yourself.

Beside Jesus Christ being able to pay His taxes, on the build-up to his crucifixion, rode on a 'brand new' colt that no man had never ridden (in our contemporary world that should be likened to the latest car), His cloth was so precious, high quality and costly that the soldiers, during His crucifixion could not tear it apart but casted lot for it.

The most interesting thing about this is, if the bible calls this a "poverty state", I can only imagine the riches Jesus handed over to us when He took our poverty.

JEHOVAH JIREH OUR PROVIDER

Furthermore, as strong as God desires to save us from sin, so is His desire to prosper us. Just like Abraham, who was very rich with cattle, silver and gold, so also, we who are the seeds of Abraham, are expected to be rich in silver, gold, cars, houses among others and be an extension of these things to others.

Moreover, it's also important to understand that every promise of God leaves us with a responsibility in order to take full delivery of it. So, in the succeeding chapters of this book, we shall be talking about what we need to do, steps to take and principles to live by so as to fully enjoy divine abundance like what the Bible promises us to. Still on that, just remember our previous example of how much Christianity is an equation by which several variables are involved in it so that we end up with a good single outcome which is prosperity. So always remember that there are the steps (variables) that are involved.

Note that life in the redemptive covenant is a glorious experience which have been fully paid for and delivered through the sacrificial death and resurrection of our Lord Jesus for our redemption and glorification.

In all these things, a willing heart, or those that are

willing to take it further than just listening to us writing, or preaching will have greater chances of reaping the rewards in the end.

We can even borrow from the words of Apostle McCurry during the delivery of the sermon on giving, that, "This (the message on giving) may not be for everybody. This is only for people who really want to be blessed."

He also went ahead and added some words on the point, stating that, "That's who (people who really want to be blessed) I want to talk to today. I want to talk to those who really want to live the blessed life that Jesus Christ died for. So, we come, the momentum of giving; so today we come to present to you the biblical principles on how to live and not to have a moment."

When we write about these things, we mention the momentum of giving in the same sentence as the 'biblical' principles. This really does not add any new dimension to the subject, but just to emphasise that indeed this is coming from God, but unfortunately not everyone is willing to take up the word and run with it so as to fully partake in the work of God which leads to a life that is prosperous.

A brief overview of what we are discussing in this book

CHAPTER ONE: GOD'S UNCONDITIONAL LOVE

The foundation and basis for all forms of giving is love. God's Love was demonstrated by what He gave. He gave His only begotten son- Jesus, the best, the greatest and the most precious that God had, for a ransom for the sins of all men. You cannot therefore, give something worthwhile to someone outside the premise and attitude of love. However, love cannot be shown to anyone without giving. You can give your talents, you can give your time or you can give your treasures, as long as it is done for the sake of sharing as Christ left us to do, then the Kingdom of God has something to gain from. PRAISE GOD!

CHAPTER TWO: DIVINE EXCHANGE RATE

This chapter aims to broaden your perspective about the biblical concept of giving. What is giving? Do you lose anything when you give? Do you desire to know the various types of giving? Are you familiar with words like tithe, offerings, first fruit and alms and you desire an in-depth understanding? However, if any of these questions apply to you; then, this chapter is included in this book to answer the questions on your heart as regards different types of biblical giving.

CHAPTER THREE: TITHES

This chapter will reveal the mystery behind the power, promise and principles of abundance and prosperity through tithing. More so, we will be sharing some personal experiences about tithing with you in this chapter to challenge and encourage you. Much more truths will be revealed to you as you read on.

CHAPTER FOUR: OFFERING

Life is about giving and receiving. Do you know that, an offering does not necessarily have to be money? God has blessed you with so much love, care, time, resources and knowledge to give. There are people whose need is healing, some, a child out of jail and others could be a need for a job. Assuredly, you can expect a reward when you give any offering. In this chapter, you will see the principle of sowing and reaping in a broader dimension.

CHAPTER FIVE: FIRST FRUIT

First fruit is an increase in income that is set apart for God as an offering. And this comes with a powerful promise from God. It is indeed an effectual way of getting the best from God. It can also serve as proof that you love God more than money. This particular topic is controversial among believers today but this chapter will broaden your knowledge about it and thereby help you to stay connected to God's divine blessing via "first fruiting".

CHAPTER SIX: ALMS

It is more blessed to give than to receive. In addition,

Jesus said, "You will always have the poor around you…" When you give alms, you are showing kindness and charity to the needy and helpless. You will see in this chapter inspiring testimonies of rewards from giving of alms. I believe that this chapter will prod you to give alms joyfully and cheerfully.

CHAPTER SEVEN: OTHER WAYS OF GIVING

Thanksgiving offering, burnt offering, grain offering, etc. are diverse means of securing divine blessings. All these forms of giving have biblical root and divine promise. This chapter will expound more about each one of them.

CHAPTER EIGHT: BENEFITS OF GIVING

God gives to us what is in His hands when we have released what is in our hand. Giving is not a loss. This is the chapter where you will find words of encouragement and motivation for purposeful and joyful giving.

CHAPTER NINE: RIGHT ATTITUDE FOR PROFITABLE GIVING

This chapter will explain the kind of attitude for acceptable giving. You might have heard that, "Attitude is everything and your attitude will always determine your altitude." It is not only what you have done that is important; the way you do it is also critical in determining the end result. Check your attitude in the light and reflection of the divine and eternal mirror of God's ever faithful word.

CHAPTER TEN: TESTIMONIALS

Testimonies are written to present all the truths revealed in this book in a conclusive, challenging and inspiring manner. This chapter will launch you to action which is the ultimate proof of faith and understanding.

Therefore, we declare that you come into a new realm where Heaven's economy is your earthly reality. I pray that the eyes of your understanding be enlightened as you delve deeper into the ocean of divine insight and revelations for prosperity and abundance through obedience to God's command to GIVE!

CHAPTER ONE

God's Love - Foundation For Giving

The foundation of any building determines the strength and nature of the building. The subject of giving cannot be fully appreciated without understanding the most important gift ever given to humanity - Jesus Christ, who paid the costliest price for the ransom of all mankind.

This is clearly described in the book of John 3:16-17, see below:

John 3:16-17 (AMPC)

16 For God so greatly loved and dearly prized the world that He [even] gave up His only begotten (unique) Son, so that whoever believes in (trusts in, clings to, relies on) Him shall not perish (come to destruction, be lost) but have eternal (everlasting) life.

17 For God did not send the Son into the world in order to judge (to reject, to condemn, to pass sentence on) the world, but that the world might find salvation and be made safe and sound through Him.

From the above scriptures, it is important to emphasize the word 'GAVE'. After the fall of man in Genesis, man was sent off the presence of God and man was ruled by the devil. We want you to take note of the word GAVE that we just highlighted in the previous sentence as it will be key to what happened between mankind and God back in the early days of life, when there was just Adam and Eve as the first to be created by God.

Humanity was hopelessly lost in the kingdom of darkness and satanic influence. The only way, God could win man back to himself was not through war with the devil or by commanding the whole world to come to Him (whereas He has the power to do so) but God began the journey into the redemption of mankind from the kingdom of darkness through the ACT OF GIVING.

This further makes us understand that the subject of giving is not a dormant force but an active force and also the potency that it carries. It is an active force that portrays the nature of God.

The common human nature can always share or even give as long as we have enough left with us, but it becomes naturally foolish when you have just one kind of a thing and u still gave it out.

St John gospel laid emphasis on the nature of what God gave. He did not give out of the many sons He has, He didn't give the least of His sons, He did not give some of His sons, but the bible says God gave His only begotten Son, the message translation of the bible put verse 16 this way:

***16** "This is how much God loved the world: He gave his Son, his one and only Son...*

God gave His only, the best, the greatest, the most precious that He had, out as a sacrifice to humanity. Praise the Lord! Giving is not just a matter of sending off some extra provisions from your pocket or house, but this is done for a cause, and no matter what you have in store, the cause becomes greater than what you think you have to an extent that you won't even mind to give away the last that you have.

God disregarded all other alternatives to saving mankind from sickness, poverty, being broke, lack, shame, begging into abundant life but chose the path of giving His one and only Son Jesus Christ. By giving His only one Son as sacrifice for us, he now has millions of sons all over the world today. Nothing ever multiplies by holding it back, if you ever want more of anything you have currently let go of it and you will gain much more.

Moreover, we should understand that love is the principal motivation behind every genuine giving as demonstrated by God, giving is the first proof of God's love for us. The whole world belongs to God and so if He needed anything He can always create it for Himself, but His love for us was the reason for giving His only Son, Jesus.

The scripture, in Romans 5:8, says, "But God shows and clearly proves His [own] love for us by the fact that while we were still sinners, Christ (the Messiah, the

Anointed One) died for us."

The love of God is so great that He gave His only Son while we were yet sinners, when we were yet messed up and out in the streets, guess what? He still came out and rescued us. He said, it doesn't matter where you are currently, when I come and give you something, it's going to be greater than what you think you have. He didn't give it to us when we were on the high; he gave it to us when we were on our lowest state because he wants to bring us up on high out of the dust into glory.

1 John 3:1 (AMPC)

See what [an incredible] quality of love the Father has given (shown, bestowed on) us, that we should [be permitted to] be named and called and counted the children of God! And so we are! The reason that the world does not know (recognize, acknowledge) us is that it does not know (recognize, acknowledge) Him.

From the above scripture we see that millions of people are called sons of God all across the world today because God demonstrated His Love by giving the one and only Son that He has, by this He gained back His Son through resurrection of Christ and also gained more sons on earth through salvation.

Nobody ever loses what they give, you only loose what you keep. Nothing increases and appreciates until it is given out of love. So, let us start demonstrating the love nature of God in us by being unrepentant givers.

When we became Christians, it might have been by choice, but for some, it was because they were forced by life which has the tendencies of pressing people into the corner most of the times. When such happens, some people tend also to look for counsel from church leaders and that is how people end up in church, becoming Christians because they would have been forced by life situations to go and look for the men of God. Even if it happens like this, God still rejoices when a single soul is added unto His Kingdom.

Now, having said the above, it comes down to when we also mention that even if you were introduced into the Kingdom of God because of life circumstances, you will now have to be a giver whilst in the House of God by your own choice. Just like we have already alluded to, God gave us His only begotten Son so that He could die for our sins by entirely His choice.

You must therefore choose to be a giver out of the love from your own heart. This is the love that we have been mentioning that it is indeed the foundation of giving.

How is love the foundation of giving? Well, it is indeed simple to understand. When you look at life, you are first moved by the feeling in your heart whenever you are looking at any situation. Now, the direction with which your heart is moved determines your next effort.

Imagine now carrying the feeling of love in you, you will be compelled to seeing something improving daily, just like when God looked down to us before Christ came, He saw a people that was lost, a people that was confused, and a lot of other poor people who did not have silver and gold, nor did they have live animals to be offering to God back in the Old Testament days for the atonement of their sins. Now because some did not have these animals to offer, it meant that when others were getting blessed, all they did was to feel sorry for themselves or give themselves away to hard labour just so that they could also participate when others did.

But a lot of things changed when Christ came down on earth. He died for everyone, just as He was given to everyone by God, His father who had been moved by love when looking at the situation that was obtaining on earth as alluded to in the previous paragraph.

All the above explains how love is the foundation of giving, you observe first, get moved by love in your heart, and because you have developed love, you act accordingly by giving out something that you believe will greatly assist in whatever that you would have observed.

Moving ahead, chapter two explains the types/modes of giving because we must understand that there are various types of giving and how we ought to appropriate them because God wants each and every one of us to walk and enjoy His financial blessings.

CHAPTER TWO

The Divine Exchange Rate

Our friends in Finance and Investment understand the exchange rate as simply the amount, or rate at which one currency can be used to buy another one other than itself. This therefore measures the power that one currency has over the other, which in turn influences a number of things like the level of the difference between exports and imports for a country, or how local businesses may have an advantage when it comes to selling their products, and, or services abroad.

We may go on and on about the above example, but we feel that we have highlighted enough to keep up with everyone, after all, this is not some investment analysis book. However, the important issue to note from the above is that the exchange rate appears to be affecting quite a number of things other than just itself. These things have been mentioned as things such as exports and imports, among others.

Therefore, what just started as the mere mention of an exchange rate end up having some impact on things of national interest and if not handled well would lead to some disastrous outcomes like a widely negative trade balance as well as weak competitiveness in regional trade, all having adverse effects on the nation at large.

Now, moving ahead, if the real exchange rate that we all understand, and belonging to us in the world, can have such an impact on life, what more then about the exchange rate that the Almighty God uses?

Well, before diving into what the exchange rate that God uses can do to us, let us first try and make everyone understand what exactly this Godly exchange rate is.

The Bible says that it is better to give than it is to receive (Acts 20:35).

Acts 20:35 (AMPC)

In everything I have pointed out to you [by example] that, by working diligently in this manner, we ought to assist the weak, being mindful of the words of the Lord Jesus, how He Himself said, It is more blessed (makes one happier and more to be envied) to give than to receive.

What does the Bible mean here when it says that it is more blessed to give than to receive? It means that when receiving, you will only enjoy that which has been placed in your hands, but when you are the one that is giving, you will end up being more blessed (having more in your hands) that the person that you would have given in the first place.

Looking at the above paragraph, we come to the simple explanation of the exchange rate that God uses –

that for very unit that you give, you are guaranteed of a tenfold, hundred-fold and even a thousand-fold more. It is as simple as that.

God's currency is therefore giving, and it is always stronger than all the other currencies that we have on earth. God is always going to give back to you in greater ways than you have given before. You make a living by what you get, we make a lifestyle by what we give. Many people live by their income we live by our outcome. EVERYTHING WE HAVE COMES FROM OUR GIVING.

Since we are in possession of God's currency, we ought to give it away because what an exchange rate means is that the rate is determined, or realized only when you exchange it for something else. And, when exchanging, you let go of what is in your *Hands*. Thus, just as been emphasized before, giving is an action, you ought to act, and the action is to give away.

I know you might wonder, what does this mean? To explain further, I'll like to ask if you have ever travelled outside of the U.S. If yes, then you will definitely realize that, when you travel abroad, your dollar is worth more compared with other country's dollar. That's something they call exchange rate. It works when comparing two currencies. In our case, we are comparing the 'currencies' of giving and receiving.

For instance, if you go to China the rate of exchange should be around one U.S. dollar to approximately six Chinese Yuan, if you go to South Africa, one U.S.

dollar equal approximately 14 South African Rands, and in Mexico, one U.S. dollar equal approximately 19 Mexican pesos, why? This is so because there's a rate of exchange that takes place among different currencies in the global market, and this rate is subject to changes in the movement of the market as determined by demand and supply, trade, politics, inflation and other factors.

Good news now, that the currency of God, that is giving, is not to be affected by any sort of external, or internal factors, it remains steadfast and all those who make use of it shall never beg of bread.

Now to the subject of different forms of GIVING, you need to understand that, there is a divine rate of exchange.

We need to change our vocabulary from, "I pay my tithe" to "I give my tithe". Just before you wonder too far about the difference between the two ways of speaking concerning your kingdom giving, you pay your Bills, you pay your taxes, you give your tithes it is a willing exchange, because if you decide not to, there is absolutely no one who is going to come knocking at your door threatening to attach your property just because you would have defaulted.

My Giving Testimony

One evening at bible study at Christian Fellowship Center, Cleveland, OH, after we had received the word it was offering time.

As I pulled out my wallet to give, I saw that all I

had was change. I was about to count it, but I said to myself that it was not necessary, God knows how much it is. So, when I went up to give, I just turned my wallet upside down and emptied it all into the offering basket. I was not aware that my pastor, Shirley McKinney, was looking at this. She stopped me and prophesied to me that because I was willing to give God all that I had, I would never be broke again in my life. Well her prophecy came true. I have never been without money since then. I have not always had a large sum of money, but I have never had a small amount either.

Give, and [gifts] will be given unto you; good measure, pressed down, shaken together, and running over, will they pour into [the pouch formed by] the bosom [of your robe and used as a bag]. For with measure you use when you confer benefits on others], it will be measured back to you.   Luke 6:38 (AMPC)

By Margie Nelson

Another insight to this can be found in proper understanding of what Jesus meant by, "It is better to give than receive". You see, it's better to give because that means when you give, you don't lose it, instead, got it!

Another way of saying this is, if you can give it that means you got it. So, it's better to give than it is to receive because "if I can't give it, it's a proof that, I don't have it." Therefore, if we want to make sure we always have it, then we need to follow the ever faithful and unbreakable principles of giving.

What is an Exchange Rate?

An exchange rate is the value of one nation's currency versus the currency of another nation or economic zone. For example, how many U.S. dollars does it take to buy one euro? In the bible each way of giving has a divine rate of exchange.

In order to fully understand what an exchange rate is, we have to explain to you different types of exchange rate systems that the countries of the world use. Read below for some of the different type of Exchange Rates

Free Floating / our TITHES

A free-floating exchange rate rises and falls due to changes in the foreign exchange market, particularly on the demand and supply variations. We always think about our tithes as a free floating promise of God; he said he would "rebuke the devourer for your sakes, and he shall not destroy the fruits of your ground; neither shall your vine cast her fruit before the time in the field, saith the LORD of hosts." When God said He would "rebuke the devourer," He promised that He would protect us from such disasters that seek to eat away all the fruits of our labor even before we have the chance to enjoy these. I am sure you know of people who work day and night only for nothing to really come out of the work of their hands.

Restricted Currencies/ our ALMS

Some countries have restricted exchange rates, limiting their currency to within the countries' borders. Also, a restricted currency can have its value set by the government on a daily basis.

That's Alms giving. With these, God sets the return for your compassion. Alms are money or goods given to those in need as an act of charity. The word alms is used many times in the King James Version of the Bible. It comes from the Old English word ælmesse and ultimately from a Greek word meaning "pity, mercy." In its original sense, when you give alms, you are dispensing mercy.

Matthew 6:1-4 (AMPC) contains four occurrences:

1. Take care not to do your good deeds publicly or before men, in order to be seen by them; otherwise you will have no reward reserved for and awaiting you] with and from your Father Who is in heaven.

2 Thus, whenever you give to the poor, do not blow a trumpet before you, as the hypocrites in the synagogues and in the streets like to do, that they may be recognized and honored and praised by men. Truly I tell you, they have their reward in full already.

3 But when you give to charity, do not let your left hand know what your right hand is doing,

*4 So that your deeds of charity may be
in secret; and your Father Who sees in secret
will reward you openly.*

Here, Jesus taught that almsgiving is for God to see, not to show off before others. Those giving out of their love for God are not to announce their giving or draw attention to it.

Onshore Vs. Offshore / OFFERING & SEED SOWING

Exchange rates can also be different for the same country. In some cases, there is an onshore rate and an offshore rate. Generally, a more favorable exchange rate can often be found within a country's border versus outside its borders. China is one major example of a country that has this rate structure. Additionally, China's yuan is a currency that is controlled by the government. Every day, the Chinese government sets a mid-point value for the currency, allowing the yuan to trade in a band. To quote The late Oral Roberts was highly influential in spreading the concept of seed faith offerings, and he taught people to expect a miracle when they sow a "seed" from their "need." He wrote, "To realize your potential, to overcome life's problems, to see your life become fruitful, multiply and provide abundance (i.e., health, prosperity, spiritual renewal, in the family or oneself), you should decide to follow the divine law of the sower and the harvest. Sow the seed of His promise in the ground of your need" (from "Principles of the Seed"). In the July 1980 edition of Abundant Life, Roberts wrote, "Solve your money needs with money seeds" (page 4). Your seed can yield you 30, 60- or 100- fold blessing

Quotation/ FIRST FRUIT

Typically, an exchange rate is quoted using an acronym for the national currency it represents. For example, the acronym USD represents the U.S. dollar, while EUR represents the Euro. To quote the currency pair for the dollar and the euro, it would be EUR/USD. In this case, the quotation is Euro to dollar, and translates to 1-Euro trading for the equivalent of $1.13 if the exchange rate is 1.13. In the case of the Japanese Yen, it's USD/JPY, or dollar to Yen. An exchange rate of 100 would mean that 1 dollar equals 100 Yen.

The movement from the midpoint of the currency pair is then called the 'spread', which determines how much the broker, or middlemen will get from selling the currency pair to interested parties, for example if 2% is the spread from the mid-point, then the middleman will be making 2% of the amount that he or she will sell to the interested party. The first fruit was given before the entire harvest was taken as a deposit or down payment guaranteeing God's blessing upon the rest of the harvest. First Fruits offering is a free will offering, separate from and in addition to your tithe. It can be given to the church or the priest.

Now let's talk about the types of giving. According to the Bible, there are four types of giving, which are, The Tithes, The First fruits, The Offerings [can also be seen as the seeds or Sowing] and then the last one is the Alms. In the following chapters, we deal with each one of them in detail, but first, here are a couple of verses from the Bible that you can use to explain a few lessons about giving.

John 3:16 (KJV)

16 For God so loved the world, that he gave his only begotten Son, that whosoever believeth in him should not perish, but have everlasting life.

Luke 6:38 (KJV)

38 Give, and it shall be given unto you; good measure, pressed down, and shaken together, and running over, shall men give into your bosom. For with the same measure that ye mete withal it shall be measured to you again.

In the message Bible, Luke 6:39(b), says, "Give away your life; you'll find life given back, but not merely given back—given back with bonus and blessing. Giving, not getting, is the way. Generosity begets generosity."

GIVING

Give and it will be given back: This speaks strongly of one of the biblical principles on how to LIVE, not just to have a moment, but have a lifestyle of perpetual blessings – "The Abundant Life"

I believe from this moment on, you will never have another broke day in your life.

Let's make a prophetic proclamation ~ Please confess with me: **I WILL NEVER BE BROKE AGAIN BECAUSE I AM A GIVER!!**

CHAPTER THREE

Tithes

Malachi 3:10 (AMPC)

Bring all the tithes (the whole tenth of your income) into the storehouse, that there may be food in My house, and prove Me now by it, says the Lord of hosts, if I will not open the windows of heaven for you and pour you out a blessing, that there shall not be room enough to receive it.

So, here comes the most difficult part about being a Christian, because, trust us, throughout our Christian lives, we have noticed how much people justify themselves out of giving their tithes. Sadly, we have heard of some ministries that do not encourage their members to give tithing at all because they have a different belief system than the rest of us. Well, from reading the above verse, it is clear that God wants us to give tithes as part of our offerings.

When you give tithing, there will be good testimonies to come out of that, read the below:

Tithing and giving

Tithing and giving is a way of life for Alvin and Helen

Copeland. They were taught the principles of tithing early on in their marriage. And that the term tithe means 10 percent of your income, and that you should cheerfully bring the tithe and offering to your local church. It is God who gives us the opportunity to work to make the tithe. What's so wonderful about tithing is that when you give the 10 percent, your remaining 90 percent seems to stretch out and cover all your financial needs. You don't have to worry about having more month than money, when you give the tithe. Over nearly 49 years of marriage, we have seen the power of consistently tithing. It's as though we have been under God's protective financial umbrella all these years. We are self-employed, and there were times when we were concerned about getting new clients. But God has been faithful and has sent new clients our way. Helen would always say, "God, if we don't have any business, we can't tithe." God has always come through with new clients and many times we have gotten new business as a result of client referrals. If you're faithful in giving the tithe, God will be faithful in meeting your needs.

Alvin and Helen Copeland.

The definition of tithe from the *Oxford Dictionary of the Christian church* explains the term as <u>"the tenth part of all fruits and profits due to God and thus to the church for the maintenance of its ministry."</u>

In addition, a theologian defined tithe as that fixed percentage of your income that you give to God in acknowledgement of his sovereignty and lordship over your substance. Awesome!

Just a quick look at the two definitions of tithes that we have given above, the Oxford definition gives mention to the tenth part of all the fruits and profits, and also the Theologian one gives mention to the giving of tithes as an acknowledgement of his sovereignty and lordship over your substance. Take note of the words 'tenth part' and 'all fruits and profits' in the former, and also the words 'lordship over your substance' in the later.

The tenth part of every fruit and profit

We are just going to put more words to this in a very short summarized from so that we do not lose you in this important subject. We all work in life, right? We do produce something on a daily basis, right? We all do, even our little children should also learn to tithe because they also do make profits from the pocket money that they get from parents. I once came across one parent who taught her daughter to always put aside money for tithing from the pocket money that she gave to her, and she did exceptionally well!

Now, what is the meaning of the tenth part? This is simple, it is not just saying it's ten per cent of your every fruit or earnings, but this is a simple math where you count your proceeds as like from one to nine, then putting aside every tenth part for tithing to the lord. This therefore means that it is not always about money, but also in the Old Testament they also offered their beasts and sheep, and all other forms of livestock as tithes, something that we can still do in this day. Hence, if you are a goat farmer, you may count your new born goat kids and if they add up to ten, you put aside the tenth one for tithing and then start over again, putting aside every tenth count for the purpose of tithing.

Involving the example of goats really does take into account the portion of the fruits in the definition of tithing because as people, we have grown to being used to monetary definitions that end up speaking of profits in monetary value as opposed to profits in the fruits of our produce.

Acknowledgement of His lordship over your substance

Again, we would like to add some few words on this one. We do know that God is sovereign and He does what He wants at any time. We also do know that God is the most powerful and can destroy or build things at any time. We also do know that God owns everything, because He says silver and gold belongs to Him.

Besides all the above, He still takes time to make sure that our lives do matter, and are lived in a good way that pleases Him and men. With Him being sovereign, He can choose to withhold His blessing on your life, and to make sure that you do not get that job, but He doesn't. With Him being the most powerful, He can choose to destroy all your property and crops in a second, but He waters them with the water from the rain and makes sure that they exist well until harvest. He just does it all for us!

Now, the reasoning behind us tithing as a sign of acknowledging his lordship over our substance is to say 'thank you lord for keeping my money and my fruits safe from the devourers.'

We may move ahead now.

Like I said earlier, "I don't PAY my tithes. I GIVE my tithes." There is a radical difference between the two terms, just hang on! You see, when I give you something that means that I love you enough to give it to you. This why, God loved us enough to give us his only begotten son we also should love Him enough to give wholeheartedly back to Him not as a form of futile repayments but in heartfelt gratitude and thankfulness for His manifold grace towards us.

Interestingly, the 'tithe' is the same for everybody in whatever tribe, race or language, but the amount is not the same, its ten percent so if I have got Ten Dollars and I give 10%, which is one dollar, you got hundred dollars you give 10% and that will be ten dollars.

It's the same, that's just the principle of tithing. We give our tithe and that's ten percent as the bible has commanded us. So, it's for the smooth running and proper maintenance of the house of God.

So, if you want to seat comfortably and be blessed by God's word while in the sanctuary. Then you need to understand that, that's what our tithes are for, so, when we give our tithes, it's because it's a commandment from the Lord, hallelujah!

Never allow anyone get you all twisted talking about tithes, saying that we are not in the Old Testament. Giving of Tithes started before the Old Testament, because the Bible recorded that Abraham tithed to Melchizedek king of Salem (Genesis 14:18-20). Let's get into the scripture and read the story.

Genesis 14:18-20 (AMPC)

18 Melchizedek king of Salem [later called Jerusalem] brought out bread and wine [for their nourishment]; he was the priest of God Most High,

19 And he blessed him and said, Blessed (favored with blessings, made blissful, joyful) be Abram by God Most High, Possessor and Maker of heaven and earth,

20 And blessed, praised, and glorified be God Most High, Who has given your foes into your hand! And [Abram] gave him a tenth of all [he had taken].

The scriptures above point us to the place and point in time when the FIRST TITHE was offered to the Priest of the highest God. The issue about tithing is not just about saying it was only meant for the times of the Old Testament, not at all. We say this just because everything that was happening in the Old Testament turned out to be like a movie trailer to the real one that was going to come with the New Testament of Christ Jesus. Therefore, when Abraham offered the tenth of everything that he had taken back then, he simply being used by God to show people that He requires them to give the tenth part of every fruit and proceeds that they make.

When it comes to our finances, we have to understand that we are just stewards over everything that God has entrusted to us. It's not our finances anyway, so when God gives us the finances and then He asks us for the 10% in return, He gives us the 90% to be able to manage it and if we manage the 90% well, He will add blessings on top of that and it'll increase. That is when you give 10% as tithe; the remaining becomes blessed, it's a principle that can never be broken.

Now a personal experience on when the Bible talks about rebuking the devourer for our sake, one time we had a washer and dryer that lasted for almost thirty-years because the Devourer was rebuked for our sake in our household.

THE TITHE IS INTRODUCED AS LAW

Leviticus 27:30-34 (AMPC)

30 And all the tithe of the land, whether of the seed of the land or of the fruit of the tree, is the Lord's; it is holy to the Lord.

31 And if a man wants to redeem any of his tithe, he shall add a fifth to it.

> *32 And all the tithe of the herd or of the flock, whatever passes under the herdsman's staff [by means of which each tenth animal as it passes through a small door is selected and marked], the tenth shall be holy to the Lord.*
>
> *33 The man shall not examine whether the animal is good or bad nor shall he exchange it. If he does exchange it, then both it and the animal substituted for it shall be holy; it shall not be redeemed.*
>
> *34 These are the commandments which the Lord commanded Moses on Mount Sinai for the Israelites.*

So, the Bible has been clear about tithes being something that really belongs to God. It also goes ahead to say that this is the commandment that God gave to Moses on Mount Sinai. And, according to the Bible, God is the same, yesterday, today and forever [Hebrews 13:8]. Therefore, His commandments also are not subject to change like what other people would try and twist your mind in some way.

OFFERINGS AND TITHES

Deuteronomy 12:5-6 (AMPC)

> *5 But you shall seek the place which the Lord your God shall choose out of all your tribes to put His Name and make His dwelling place, and there shall you come;*

6 And there you shall bring your burnt offerings and your sacrifices, your tithes and the offering of your hands, and your vows and your freewill offerings, and the firstlings of your herd and of your flock.

In following God's word, there are rewards that always follow. In the scripture above, we see God's people being instructed to give different kinds of offerings, including tithes to the lord. Always remember that this is a matter of what God commanded us to do, and not whether we want to give or not. We have read from the previous chapters in the Bible where it says that when someone decides to withhold the tithes, he or she shall have to pay with an extra fifth on top of what they were supposed to be paying in the first place.

Now going back to the rewards, or what follows giving on God's command, we can read further from the book of Deuteronomy once again:

Deuteronomy 12:7 & 12:11-12 (AMPC)

7 And there you shall eat before the Lord your God, and you shall rejoice in all to which you put your hand, you and your households, in which the Lord your God has blessed you.

11 Then there shall be a place which the Lord your God shall choose to cause His

Name [and His Presence] to dwell there; to it you shall bring all that I command you: your burnt offerings, your sacrifices, your tithes and what the hand presents [as a first gift from the fruits of the ground], and all your choicest offerings which you vow to the Lord.

12 And you shall rejoice before the Lord your God, you and your sons and your daughters, and your menservants and your maidservants, and the Levite that is within your towns, since he has no part or inheritance with you.

Verses 7 and 12 of Deuteronomy chapter 12 now speak of how people will end up eating and rejoicing, the key term there being AFTER they have offered of their first fruits and tithing to the lord their God. This therefore means that it is indeed true that tithing is a foundation that you lay for your products to be well-protected and that your produce and inheritance will be kept safe from all forms of devourers.

BRINGING IN THE TITHE

2 Chronicles 31:4–5 (AMPC)

4 He commanded the people living in Jerusalem to give the portion due the priests and Levites, that they might [be free to] give themselves to the Law of the Lord.

5 As soon as the command went abroad, the Israelites gave in abundance the firstfruits of grain, vintage fruit, oil, honey, and of all the produce of the field; and they brought in abundantly the tithe of everything.

In the above scripture, we see a happy nation that did not hesitate to bring in a lot of offerings for the lord their God. Verse 5 ends up by saying that they brought in abundantly the tithe of everything. I do like the use of the term 'everything' here, which takes us back to our previous Oxford definition of tithes, where we spoke of giving the tenth of every fruit and proceeds being given to God – this means everything!

You Tithes belong to your local church were you are being feed the word of God and in faithfulness to bless everyone who obeys His command to tithe even in the times of need.

We have spoken of how God is able to keep his word and deliver all His promises when we said that he never changes. He is not just there to be dishing out instructions like some angry earthly father who has no clue how to reward his children on good behaviour and love. Ours is a heavenly Father who loves us and will make sure that He leads us to greener pastures when we rightly obey His word and be cheerful givers.

We have already spoken about the foundation of giving being love, and we will notice that God rewards those that believe in His word such that they love His church and thus would not hesitate to give their tithes for the sake of the Kingdom of God.

In the testimony below, the people involved did not hesitate to give when called upon because they love God. God saw this and He rewarded them with good things and now they rejoice in their lives, just like as we have mentioned before when reading from the book of Deuteronomy chapter 12.

If it's God's will, it is God's bill

Prove Me Now

"Faithfully pay your titles and I will faithfully meet your every need." That was the Word that I received in 2017 that changed my life. I decided to fully trust God with my greatest struggle and that was trusting him with my finances. From that day forth I obediently paid my tithes faithfully. I assumed that I could not afford to pay titles and keep my family afloat financially but God Proved His Word to Me.

There has been absolutely no lack, in fact we began to walk in the overflow. We lived in a house that was too small for our family and God blessed us with the home of our dreams. We drove in a 7-passenger car, with 8 kids, and He blessed us with a 12-passenger vehicle. We needed new furniture and beds for our new house and God blessed us with an entire house of new furniture FREE of charge. My children needed to be healed and they were healed. I needed family member saved and He saved. We had NO money in the bank and now we have savings.

Once I trusted Him with my tithe, He proved to me

that He had an open heaven awaiting to flood me with everything I needed in excess and overflow.

Nichelle N. Daniels, MIT

Below is also another testimony about the goodness of God when people decide to live their lives whilst giving tithes to God.

The Devourer Has Been Rebuked!!!

At a very young age, my Grandmother, the famous Lou Betty Goldsby taught me how to tithe and be a giver. I never realized that she was setting me up for blessing for the rest of my life. Even back in the day when I was getting a mere 321.00 a month, my Grandmother encouraged me to tithe. She instructed me that the 10th didn't belong to me it belonged to God. As I got older I tried not to stray from that principle but as life happens well...so I thought in my finite wisdom that I would stop tithing just until I get caught with my bills. Well that day never came. Until I finally decided to return to the wisdom instilled in me for so long did things turn around.

As a result, I kept a car for ten years and never put anything but oil, gas, tires, and brakes on it, and when I tell you I drove the wheels off this car and it was two years old when I purchased the car. I have never gone without anything I needed. I've had three cars stolen just to get restored immediately and to get something better each time. When other people I worked with lost their jobs, mine was spared. I have had supernatural favor on my job that opened doors O never imagined. Even my life was spared in 2012 when I had a stroke and suffered no effects other than the evidence they could see on the x-rays. A neurologist in the field for thirty years was baffled by my case but I know it was God rebuking the devourer for my sake because I give him back what he has asked me for.

Pastor Denise Washington

In God and in giving there are always testimonies to preach of the goodness of the Lord. Praise Him!
NEHEMIAH REESTABLISHES THE TITHE
Kindly read the below and see how Nehemiah had to write about tithes as a form of offering.

Nehemiah 10:35-37 (AMPC)

35 And [we obligate ourselves] to bring the firstfruits of our ground and the first of all the fruit of all trees year by year to the house of the Lord,

36 As well as the firstborn of our sons and of our cattle, as is written in the Law, and

> *the firstlings of our herds and flocks, to bring to the house of our God, to the priests who minister in [His] house.*
>
> *37 And we shall bring the first and best of our coarse meal, our contributions, the fruit of all kinds of trees, of new wine, and of oil to the priests, to the chambers of the house of our God. And we shall bring the tithes from our ground to the Levites, for they, the Levites, collect the tithes in all our rural towns.*

In verse 37, there is the mention of the best of our 'coarse' meal, and we are interested in the word 'best.' Here, the narrative is that when giving to God, we ought not to be found trying to give him only the left-overs when we had already taken the best out of our harvest, that is not the way God wants it. When giving to God, it has to be the best part of what we have, remember one of the testimonials above, where one believer among us had actually to empty the wallet into the offering basket, and indeed God was delighted at seeing this.

You therefore do not tithe because you have something to spare, you rather tithe because God would have blessed you with the best and hence you will take from the best and into the House of the lord.

CHAPTER FOUR

Offerings

The next type of giving that we are going to be discussing is-offering. You need to understand that, when you give your offering, what you are releasing is your seed, for a bountiful harvest.

The word seed and sowing are all synonymous, they are all interchangeable. There is something to note about seeds. When you place a seed into the soil, first, it must die, so that the plant can grow out of it.

Therefore, whenever you plant a seed, that seed is dying out of your hands while you're giving it to somebody else. However, it will surely grow out as a plant which bears fruits in multiple folds of the quantity of seeds planted.

Yes! You cannot find any reasonable farmer who has ever planted a seed without expecting to receive a harvest. So, if that's the case, when you give your offering; you are in the 'growing' business; you cannot miss your harvest.

Understandably, if I'm a farmer and I'm planting seeds; I'll have an expectation to receive my harvest. Likewise, if you are planting financial seeds; you need to name that seed, so you can receive that particular harvest, You will agree with me that, not everyone needs money. Someone may need a healing, another may need their mind regulated, another needs to get a child out of jail you name that seed and when you name that seed, you have the expectation for that harvest.

So, I need you to understand that, the inspiration behind sowing seed of offering is reward. So, when you give, you should expect a reward for your giving.

Finally, on seed sowing and offerings, let's study Matthew 13:3- 8 and in the Bible these words are in red which means, they are not my words. They are Jesus' words instead!

Matthew 13-3-8 (AMPC)

3 And He told them many things in parables (stories by way of illustration and comparison), saying, A sower went out to sow.

4 And as he sowed, some seeds fell by the roadside, and the birds came and ate them up.

5 Other seeds fell on rocky ground, where they had not much soil; and at once they sprang up, because they had no depth of soil.

6 But when the sun rose, they were scorched, and because they had no root, they dried up and withered away.

7 Other seeds fell among thorns, and the thorns grew up and choked them out.

8 Other seeds fell on good soil, and yielded grain—some a hundred times as much as was sown, some sixty times as much, and some thirty.

So according to Matthew 13:3 – 8; we can get 30, 60 and a 100-foldblessing on our offerings. However, note that, this does not apply to your tithe, first fruit or alms. The 30, 60 and a 100-fold blessing only applies to your offering, which is also your seed to sow for bountiful harvest.

It is important you understand this because it will help your understanding of the rate of exchange that takes place in every kind of giving.

It is not always for you

I want remind you that God has called you not only to be blessed but to also be a blessing. Therefore, another important reality is, sometimes when someone gives you an offering, a seed; it doesn't mean that you have to consume or use the offering for yourself. On the contrary, God may be passing through you to someone else, who desperately needs that seed. You need to discern the bread from the seed; what to keep from what to give to the other person and what to eat from what to sow

The bible says,

For as the rain and snow come down from the heavens, and return not there again, but water the earth and make it bring forth and sprout, that it may GIVE SEED TO THE SOWER AND BREAD TO THE EATER.
- **Isaiah55:10** (AMPC)

I remember one time, somebody gave me $200 and when they gave me the $200, I was excited, but I knew instantly it wasn't mine. I KNEW INSTANTLY THAT IT WASN'T MINE!! So, I took the $200 and I put it in an envelope and had it in my purse, I was just waiting for the opportunity to sow the seed because I knew it wasn't mine so then almost a week went by and I was feeling like – WHO IS THIS $200 FOR? so then one of my clients came to the salon for her weekly hair service and she was a faithful client. I've been servicing her for years and she was telling me that her lights were going to get cut off.

The Holy Spirit said THAT'S WHO IT'S FOR, that's who it's for. So, then as she got to talking and explaining her situation, once I was done servicing her and she was about to go, and I said hold on I got a little something for you and then I went and got the envelope out of my bag and gave it to her , she looked on with curiosity in her eyes as she opened the envelope and she just stood there crying. So, every time you receive a seed that doesn't mean that the seed is for you. As a sower you have to wait and see, who is the seed for, amen!

Be prepared for every opportunity to sow

The truth is, if you really are a 'sower', you just want to have a certain compartment in your wallet. I have it in my phone and it's a seed. So, it's a $20 bill folded up, tucked away on the side of my phone. So, I'm prepared and waiting for an opportunity to bless somebody whether it's in the grocery store or any other place.

For instance, if you're behind somebody and they are contemplating not getting groceries, then they tell the cashier "you know what I got to put these groceries back." You may have to reach out and say something like, "Oh! No, you don't have to". Then you reach into your 'seed wallet' and offer to pay for their bills.

I really like the idea of the seed wallet, because like a warrior in God's army, you are always ready to give.

This is an acceptable offering and seed; you can expect to reap the harvest in many folds. Praise God!

Here is a Testimony on God's faithfulness to bless everyone who obeys His command to give tithe and offerings cheerfully.

"I have tapped into the overflow blessings of God"

"I have been a proud member of New Beginnings Ministry for two years and my life has been enriched in so many ways. But most of all I have tapped into the overflow blessings of God, through the awesome teaching of tithes and offering.

As a Christian, I have always been a giver and blessed God with my tithes and offering. But, with the combination teaching of Apostle Gregory McCurry and Pastor Teresa McCurry my life was overtaken with blessings.

Apostle Gregory McCurry started pouring into my life that I was already a winner and my record is 365-0. He explained that, as I remain connected to God; I will receive the Amos 9:13-15 blessing. This states that, "Yes indeed, it won't be long now, God's decree. Things are going to happen so fast your head will swim one thing fast on the heels of the other. You won't be able to keep up. Everything will be happening at once and everywhere you look blessings! Blessings like wine pouring off the mountains and hills. I'll make everything right again for my people." (MSG Bible)

Secondly, Pastor Teresa McCurry perfectly illustrated the true principles of tithing and different offerings to tap into the abundance of God.

To begin with; I personally did not know there were four different types of "giving" in the bible. Namely: Tithes, offering, first fruit and alms.

As soon as I discovered this, I immediately activated all the four types if giving into my life through meditation in order to change my thinking process totally.

Consequently, before I knew it the blessings of God had overtaken my life and my home! There has not been any form of lack and I have given more to God than I ever have since my twenty-two years of salvation.

Since my membership in 2016 at New Beginnings Ministry, I have received financial blessings, a newer vehicle, and have been on seven vacations just to name a few.

I'm grateful because, the McCurry's did not make up "Hocus Pocus" numbers to drum up monies from the people of God. Instead, they simply teach the word of God in love so that everyone can understand and receive everything God desires for His children.

Angela Hunter

Ephesians 5:20 (KJV)

Giving thanks always for all things unto God and the Father in the name of our Lord Jesus Christ;

"Failing to be thankful can be likened to a friend opening up his home to serve you a wonderful dinner. Then after you've eaten, you jump up from the dinner table, never thanking the person who prepared the food or showing any appreciation for being invited to share a special time in his home." Bishop Bill Mckinney

Offering is all about giving thanks for what has already been dome for you. In the case with God, if you thank Him for what He has already done, He will also reward you with more good things, which is something worth praising Him for.

We will continue reading from the Bible and learn more about offering:

2 Corinthians 9:7 (AMPC)

Let each one [give] as he has made up his own mind and purposed in his heart, not reluctantly or sorrowfully or under compulsion, for God loves (He takes pleasure in, prizes above other things, and is unwilling to abandon or to do without) a cheerful (joyous, "prompt to do it") giver [whose heart is in his giving].

Praise the Lord for the scripture that we are about to read below:

"Give, and [gifts] will be given to you; good measure, pressed down, shaken together, and running over, will they pour into [the pouch formed by] the bosom [of your robe and used as a bag]. For with the measure you deal out [with the measure you use when you confer benefits on others], it will be measured back to you."
Luke 6:38 (AMPC)

We would also like to read the above verse together with Proverbs 11:24 before we explain just a few things in a few words for the benefit of everyone who is following this story. We want you to get to the end well-versed with giving knowledge.

Proverbs 11:24 (AMPC)

There are those who [generously] scatter abroad, and yet increase more; there are those who withhold more than is fitting or what is justly due, but it results only in want.

Interesting read indeed. Looking at the above two verses, we notice that there is a great deal of emphasis on the fact that you simply get out what you Put in. Remember we spoke about tithing being just a ten per cent of anything that you make, and that this ten percent will not be the same for everyone since some people earn way less than the others.

However, overall giving is not just about one type of offering, but there are others like alms and first fruits. With these, you have the freedom to increase the scale with which you give by and thus attract great blessings from God.

Luke 6:38 mentioned that you will be given using the exact same measure that you would have used by giving, and this has nothing to do with the required ten percent for tithing, but has all to do with all other types of offering.

More so, proverbs 11:24 mentioned that the people that love to give generously see themselves with more increase in their hands, yet those who are in the habit of withholding more for themselves always end up in need. This is simply to say even if these people had goodies in the beginning, the fact that they would not have shared with others results in them living in need because they would not have been blessed with a good measure, as the one they would have used to give with – they simply do not have any measure to be measured with in terms of giving.

Matthew 6:19-21 (AMPC)

19 Do not gather and heap up and store up for yourselves treasures on earth, where moth and rust and worm consume and destroy, and where thieves break through and steal.

20 But gather and heap up and store for yourselves treasures in heaven, where neither moth nor rust nor worm consume and destroy, and where thieves do not break through and steal;

21 For where your treasure is, there will your heart be also.

Now, this scripture does well in supporting what we have discussed in Chapter one, where we mentioned that giving has its foundations in love. Do you realise how Matthew mentions that your heart is right where your treasure is?

Well, we give in the Kingdom of God because we are His children and we love Him. Having loved Him, we have a home that is prepared for us in Heaven, and in this Home, nothing will be eaten by moths, nor will grasshoppers come to destroy our treasure stored up there. This then is what really manifests here on earth, on us, when we decide to give our tithes and offerings as God will then move to protect our fruits from any form of devourers.

A Heart of Gratitude

2017 was the official year to launch this including the launching of my business but also the launching of my faith. The year started off slow with no contracts, but I trusted the Lord to provide because I stepped out in faith to pursue the business that he called me to. This was a season where I could not afford to spend excess funds because it would've put my family in a tight bind. However, the Lord had spoken to my heart to give from a place of love to New Beginnings Ministries. I remembered a conversation with Pastor Teresa when she shared with me all the great things the church was doing and how they were trusting the Lord to pay the mortgage. At that moment, I had purposed in my heart to pay one month of the churches' mortgage payment. After giving an offering to New Beginnings ministry, which was the equivalent to the 1-month mortgage, I was blessed. I was blessed to give an offering that I knew would impact generations and people who come to the church to receive ministry.

I believe that I was blessed because of my heart towards giving the offering, and not necessarily the amount of the offering. A few months after giving the offering I was able to receive two major contracts that significantly shifted my income. I was so grateful to the Lord for blessing me at my time of need. I believe that blessings come in different ways and I was glad to receive my financial blessing.

~ Yolanda D. Hamilton

CHAPTER FIVE

First Fruit

Now, let's talk about another peculiar type of giving- First fruit. This is when you give God the first 'fruit' or 'produce' of your increase. It is about putting God first by giving the best and the first to Him.

The bible says;

Proverbs 3:9-10 (AMPC)

9 Honor the Lord with your capital and sufficiency [from righteous labors] and with the firstfruits of all your income; 10 So shall your storage places be filled with plenty, and your vats shall be overflowing with new wine.

As a matter of fact, back in biblical days they used to have harvest because they were farmers, or they herded cattle and other animals. So, the first born of the calf would be offered to the priest or the first harvest of the increase would be donated to the church.

In our contemporary time what would be our first fruit? The first fruit is our increase as we said earlier, yours could be your first pay check, your first bonus on your job, can be your first fruit, or Salary for the promotion or a new job you got or for the first month of a new year, once I heard the teaching I started off with my first tips, than my first day's work earnings before I knew I was first fruit my first pay check. I really got into first fruiting

Note this; the inspiration behind first fruiting is faith, generosity, gratitude and reverence to God. You see, when I 'first fruit'; I am showing God my gratitude for His blessings and regard for His position as the 'provider' in my life.

In the same vein, I am saying, "God, I trust you with my finances, I trust you with everything that I have. I am not going to hold my gift back from you"

Permit me to make a quick clarification. You see, a lot of people say money is the root of all evil, that's not true, What the scripture says in first Timothy chapter 6: 10 is *"For the LOVE of money is the root of ALL KINDS of evil for which some has strayed in the faith because of greediness"*

The evil associated with money here has to do with the stingy and self-centered attitude that some people express when they desire to keep everything that they've got for themselves.

Firstfruits was a Jewish feast held in the early spring at the beginning of the grain harvest. It was observed on Nissan 16, which was the third day after Passover and the second day of the Feast of Unleavened

Bread. Firstfruits was a time of thanksgiving for God's provision.

Leviticus 23:9-14 (AMPC)

9 And the Lord said to Moses,

10 Tell the Israelites, When you have come into the land I give you and reap its harvest, you shall bring the sheaf of the firstfruits of your harvest to the priest.

11 And he shall wave the sheaf before the Lord, that you may be accepted; on the next day after the Sabbath the priest shall wave it [before the Lord].

12 You shall offer on the day when you wave the sheaf a male lamb a year old without blemish for a burnt offering to the Lord.

13 Its cereal offering shall be two-tenths of an ephah of fine flour mixed with oil, an offering made by fire to the Lord for a sweet, pleasing, and satisfying fragrance; and the drink offering of it [to be poured out] shall be of wine, a fourth of a hin.

14 And you shall eat neither bread nor parched grain nor green ears, until this same day when you have brought the offering of your God; it is a statute forever throughout your generations in all your houses.

We shall also read more from the book of Exodus so as to gain more insight on this same subject of first fruits:

Exodus 23:16 (AMPC)

Also you shall keep the Feast of Harvest [Pentecost], [acknowledging] the firstfruits of your toil, of what you sow in the field. And [third] you shall keep the Feast of Ingathering [Booths or Tabernacles] at the end of the year, when you gather in the fruit of your labors from the field.

The Bible further has this to say about the first fruits, according to the instructions from God:

Exodus 34: 22 (AMPC)

You shall observe the Feast of Weeks, the firstfruits of the wheat harvest, and the Feast of Ingathering at the year's end.

The first fruits offering is never directly applied to Christian giving in the New Testament. However, Paul taught the Corinthian believers to set aside a collection "on the first day of the week", we have found the practice of first fruit giving to be a blessing to us and others.

"Honor the LORD with your possessions, and with the first fruits of all your increase; so your barns will be filled with plenty, and your vats will overflow…" (Proverbs 3:9–10 NKJV).

God showed us FIRST FRUITS is the KEY.

[1 Corinthians 16:2]. And, just as the offering of first fruits was an occasion of thanksgiving, so the Christian is to give with gladness. Giving should result in celebration and not sorrow.

In summary, first fruits symbolize God's harvest of souls, it illustrates giving to God from a grateful heart, and it sets a pattern of giving back to Him the first (and the best) of what He has given us.

A testimonial

I am eternally grateful to Apostle Gregory and Pastor Teresa McCurry for the astronomical impact they have in my life.

Every time we meet it is an encounter the leaves me greater because of their absolute Excellence. They are 5-Star, First Class and Top Shelf all the way.

I never leave their presence without being enriched, encouraged and energized for what's next.

You CANNOT be around them without being profoundly influenced by their Greatness, and yet they are the epitome of what it means to be humble and integral and the same time. Any time, money, or energy invested in them or any endeavour they host or sponsor will be a life changing event you will be grateful to have been a part of.

Elder Natasha Williams

My friend, you don't want to be greedy, rather; you want to show to God that you love Him with your first fruit. Now let's talk about the last kind of giving-Giving Alms.

CHAPTER SIX

Alms

Alms giving or giving of alms is an act of charity. According to the Bible charity is known as alms and when you give alms, the inspiration behind giving it is generosity. In other words, compassion in your heart drives you when you see somebody that has a need and you therefore reciprocate as directed by the scripture.

Therefore, alms in the Greek word mean pity, mercy; when we give alms, we are dispensing mercy to somebody else. So, when you see somebody on the freeway with a sign that says we WILL WORK FOR FOOD, and you give him some money, that's considered as giving alms. In Acts 3: 2, a story is told of the man who sat begging for alms at the gate called Beautiful. It reads, "*And a certain man, lame from his mother's womb was carried, whom they laid daily at the gate of the temple which is called Beautiful, to ask alms of them that entered into the temple.*"

Alms are a charitable donation and the motivation behind alms is compassion and according to the scriptures; when you give alms God will give it back to you. That is, whatever you give in alms, the scripture says God will give that back to you. Not the 30, 60 and

100-fold. He is going to give you back what you gave as it relates to alms therefore; you need to understand the exchange rate as we have discussed earlier.

Evidently, there is one exchange rate for tithes, one exchange rate for offering, one exchange rate for first fruit and another exchange rate for alms. We are therefore encouraged to always give alms.

Matthew 6:1-4 points out something very profound, kindly read below:

Matthew 6:1-4 (AMPC)

Take care not to do your good deeds publicly or before men, in order to be seen by them; otherwise you will have no reward [reserved for and awaiting you] with and from your Father Who is in heaven.

2 Thus, whenever you give to the poor, do not blow a trumpet before you, as the hypocrites in the synagogues and in the streets like to do, that they may be recognized and honoured and praised by men. Truly I tell you, they have their reward [c]in full already.

3 But when you give to charity, do not let your left hand know what your right hand is doing,

4 So that your deeds of charity may be in secret; and your Father Who sees in secret will reward you openly.

These verses admonish us to give alms out of a cheerful and loving heart without expecting the praise of any man and God who sees in secret will openly reward you.

Finally, I want you to remember that, God desires to see His children prosper in every area of their lives; however, He still wants to see how generous, grateful and reverent we are because of his blessings unto us.

Here is another powerful testimony to God's faithfulness to all that obey His command to give and not hold back!

Proverbs 19:1 (AMPC)

Better is a poor man who walks in his integrity than a rich man who is perverse in his speech and is a [self-confident] fool.

Reading ahead, the Bible, in Isaiah 58 also has something to add on to this subject:

Isaiah 58:7 (AMPC)

Is it not to divide your bread with the hungry and bring the homeless poor into your house—when you see the naked, that you cover him, and that you hide not yourself from [the needs of] your own flesh and blood?

Reading from the above, we learn that sometimes ignoring the word of God, especially on the subject of giving may render you a fool, no matter how rich you may appear to be. The Bible emphasises on how noble it is when the rich really do give and share what they have with the poor, including clothing the 'man' that they would have found naked.

Looking at the above, being a Christian is thus a matter of showing actions that are in line with the word of God on a continued basis. In the verse from proverbs 19, a poor man is said to be better than the one who is rich yet lacks integrity. Thus, avoiding tithing when the word of God encourages Christians to do so may be looked at as the lack of integrity.

Isaiah 58:10 (AMPC)

And if you pour out that with which you sustain your own life for the hungry and satisfy the need of the afflicted, then shall your light rise in darkness, and your obscurity and gloom become like the noonday.

"Give to him who asks of you, and do not turn away from him who wants to borrow from you." Matthew 5:42

Giving should be something that you take pleasure in. Remember that as we continue to share a number of scriptures here so that you know how important it is to God that you share what you have with those that are in need. However, when giving to the need, this has to be done for the glory of God, and not for yours [Matthew 6:1-4].

As we close this chapter, here is a story that corroborates giving of Alms:

> *"I was asking God about, how to know for SURE that I am hearing His voice and not my own."*

I work second shift at a hospital in Radiology. However, before going to work my daughter asked me for $60 to pay for her school fees. I ran to the bank and withdrew the $80.

You see, I wasn't really listening to her I just knew my child asked me for money to pay for her school fees so when I gave her $80 she said, "Mom it's only $60" and I realized I took too much out of my account so I put that $20 in my pocket for later if I need it. I then headed into work to start my shift.

Now, I'll like to share that, when I'm driving to and from work that is one of my times I talk to God and listen to worship music. On this wonderful occasion, I was asking God about, how to know for SURE that I am hearing His voice and not my own. Because I hear my own voice in my head that tells me to do things (at this time I was unsure if it was myself or God). I get to work and had a very busy day! After work I'm ready to get home, relax and get out of my uniform.

As I was driving home, I heard, 'go to the gas station by the hotel'. It was clear and loud *but it was repeated to me again. So, I said ok Lord if this is you, I will go but what am I to do there? Now, I live in Twinsburg, Ohio, so there are only 3 gas stations by the main roads. So, I go to the gas station by the hotel and God said wait for a man to show up and give him $20, he will tell me who and what message to give him. By this time, waiting 2 minutes seemed like 5 hours! So, I started to doubt myself saying this is nonsense, go home, you had a long busy day at work, this is not safe; but I started looking around to see if a homeless man was walking to the gas station. After 6-8 minutes of waiting, God said GO to the other gas station up the street now!*

There was a 2nd gas station next to a bigger hotel, so I drove over to it. As I parked my car, I saw a young man about 25 years old coming out of the store with oil to pour into his car, so he lifted his hood up and started pouring the oil. God said that is him! Give him $20 and tell him the message. I was surprised because I thought it was for a homeless man.

At this point I'm scared, nervous and heart pounding, but I said excuse me Sir, Do you believe in God? He replied Yes. I said I believe *in God also and he told me to tell you this: That God loves him and he hears everything you asked him for just stay focused on God and not others. Then I gave him the $20. The young man's face was like a deer in headlights!!! He said "WOW this is crazy! Ma'am can I tell you something? I live with my pregnant girlfriend and we just paid our rent but we are $20 short on our light bill. I was just asking God how am I going to pay it?!? I can't believe this!"*

We both started praising God! I told him how I just asked God if I really hear his voice and how he had me take an extra $20 out of my account this morning already knowing it was for him even though I had no clue. That day God blessed that young man and me with giving him $20, faith and hope. And I received confirmation that I do hear him, trust and faith as well. God is Amazing!!!

~ Ms. Delicia Mayes R.T. (R) (MR).

CHAPTER SEVEN

Other Ways Of Giving

3 John 1:2 (AMPC)

Beloved, I pray that you may prosper in every way and [that your body] may keep well, even as [I know] your soul keeps well and prospers.

Indeed, God wants us to prosper in all our ways, which is the reason why He has given us all these options to give offerings to Him, in a way that will invoke His blessings towards us.

In the previous chapters, we have touched on the most common types of giving that we read a lot about from the Bible scriptures, including how we can make use of the options in different ways. This way, by revealing that there are as many ways to give to God, we revealed that not a single person is to be left out, nor should be heard complaining that the only way that he or she could give, either in the House of God or to the poor, you can give you time, you can give you talents or you can give your treasures.

We can all give God has blessed us in many ways and we should desire to give back to the kingdom of God.

Moving on to the other forms of giving, the Old Testament can be said to revolve around a system of sacrificial offerings, just as outlined below:

Burnt Offering - The purpose of the Burnt Offering was for general atonement of sin and expression of devotion to God. Lev 1:3-17.

Grain Offering -a voluntary expression of devotion to God, Leviticus 2.

Peace Offering - to consecrate a meal together in fellowship of peace and a commitment to each other's future prosperity.

The modern idea of a peace offering, also known as a fellowship offering, is that of "a propitiatory or conciliatory gift." A man who offends his wife will often visit a florist with the thought that bringing home flowers will help smooth things over—the bouquet will be a "peace offering" of sorts. Propitiate means "to make someone pleased or less angry by giving or saying something desired," and conciliatory means "intended to placate or pacify."

Thanksgiving Offerings (Leviticus 7:12)

With thanksgiving offering, it is often used to give thanks to God for the good things that He would have done for you. Back in the Old Testament, they used to give their animals as a sacrifice to God, but in this day, you also do not have to worry about not having beasts to offer to Him, but you can also use anything, especially a part of what you are thanking Him for. An example is when you offer money just because He would have blessed you with a promotion at work where you will be earning more money.

Freewill Offerings (Leviticus 7:16), The free will (or freewill) offering was a sacrifice regulated by God's standards in the Mosaic Law, but it was completely voluntary (Leviticus 23:38). In the Law, the free will offering was to be of a male bull, sheep, or goat with no physical deformities or blemishes, and it was not to have been purchased from a foreigner (Leviticus 22:17–25).

Wave Offerings (Leviticus 7:30).

These offerings were completed on fire and also using the fat and breast part of the animal that would have been killed for the sacrifice. The fat was to be waved before the Lord as part of the peace offering. In this day, when one meets a stranger and wants to attack assuming animosity, in order for the next part to signal that all is well, they do wave and usually if the other part is not aiming to do any arm, would back down as a sign that peace is going to prevail between them.

Therefore, wave offerings can be a sign of peace between the people and God.

Sin Offering- an offering of atonement for unintentional sin (4:2-3, 4:20). A sin offering was a sacrifice, made according to the Mosaic Law, which provided atonement for sin. The Hebrew phrase for "sin offering" literally means "fault offering." The sin offering was made for sins committed in ignorance, or unintentional sins. The ritualistic method of the sin offering and the animal to be offered varied depending on the status of the sinner.

Heave offering - This "heaved" portion was set apart for use by the priests (Leviticus 7:34).

A heave offering was a way of presenting one's offering to God, and it appears in the Old Testament along with burnt offerings, grain offerings, freewill offerings, and the offering of the firstborn of the flocks. The heave offering is part of the Mosaic Law and was one of the common sacrifices or offerings given to God by the Israelites.

Trespass offering or guilt offering is described in Leviticus 5:14-19; 7:1-7; and 14:12-18. Two practical instances that would require a guilt offering are described in Leviticus 19:20-22 (a man sleeping with a slave who is engaged to another man) and Numbers 6:9-12 (a Nazarite who accidentally violates his vows). This offering should not be confused with the sin offering.

The trespass/guilt offering was required when a person unintentionally violated some of the Lord's holy things. "Holy things" would normally refer to things that had been dedicated to the Lord—anything from the sanctuary itself to the portion of the offerings that were normally reserved for the priests.

How this could happen inadvertently is not spelled out, but perhaps a person forgot to fulfil a vow, made some mistake in the fulfilling of it, accidently ate food that was reserved for the priests, or mistakenly ate a firstborn animal from his own flock.

CHAPTER EIGHT

Benefits Giving

So far, much has been learned about giving- the various kinds of giving and why it is so important.
However, you might ask, why give, when I have to let go of what is mine to gain nothing in return? The truth is, your giving should be for the sake of God's kingdom and not for the gain afterward because, the benefits that is attached to it will come, when the motive for giving is kingdom bond. Whatever you do for the kingdom of God comes with great benefits. But, desire for benefits after giving should not be the sole motive for us to do so.

God is not in need of anything. As a matter of fact, He [God] said in the Bible;

Psalm 50:10 (AMPC)

For every beast of the forest is Mine, and the cattle upon a thousand hills or upon the mountains where thousands are.

It will interest you to know that you and everything you have in your possession are a product of God's blessing upon you. You steward them because God blessed you with them. How then will you withhold anything you have from God who owns them all?

Surely, nobody does God a favour by giving. But when you give, it is you who becomes the beneficiary of God's favour; because giving attracts God's favour, mercy and more of God's blessing.

We gave away a used car; God responded by giving us a new one. He sent people to pay my car instalments each and every month.

We moved and gave away all our furniture. God blessed us with all new furniture, one room at a time, until our whole house was fully furnished.

This is true testimony that the harvest is always bigger than the seed.

Here in this chapter, we will be looking at the exceedingly great benefit that awaits every giver, it is in giving that you will receive. Even Jesus Christ gave His life in order to receive us.

Assuredly, it is in giving what is in your hand that releases what is in God's hand for you. When you give, you become open to receiving. This is what many people do not understand. My question to you now is, what exactly do you desire from God? Do not let it remain a desire in your heart. Act on your desire today by giving that which is commensurate to your desire. Giving has been a principle that had existed for a long time before this present generation.

Giving has always existed before the law

Truthfully, the concept of 'giving' is not just a practice that started in the New Testament era but it has started even before the law was written. The Bible recorded that Cain was the first to give an offering to God out of the fruit of the ground and his brother Abel did likewise but his brother's offering was accepted by God because, like we have mentioned before, Cain gave to God what was of a low standard than his brother, Abel who made sure to offer to God what was the best from his produce.

The principle of giving-Tithe (Don't rob God)

Quickly, let me remind you that a principle is an established rule of nature or a fundamental belief, which when followed appropriately, produces the desired results. As principles govern nature, so then, biblical principles govern the believer's daily Christian life. One of the biblical principles is the principle of giving and receiving; the analogy of sowing and reaping.

"GIVE, and it shall be GIVEN UNTO YOU; good measure, pressed down, and shaken together, and running over, shall men give into your bosom. For with the same measure that ye mete withal it shall be measured to you again." Luke 6: 38

The Bible is so clear on the principle of giving and receiving, as spelt out by the words of Jesus. (Luke 6:38 is about forgiveness but the principle is the same) There's no better way to abundance than giving out of that which you have for the furtherance of God's kingdom.

However, we discussed in our previous chapter about the kinds and modes of giving, where we briefly talked about the term, 'tithe'. You still remember, right? Okay!

Right now, in this current chapter, we are going to further our understanding to what happens when we tithe because tithing is a principle of giving, which has been laid down for everyone to follow. Before we go anymore further from here, permit me to show to you from the bible, something significant about tithing;

"Will a man rob God? Yet you have robbed me! But you say, 'In what way have we robbed you?' In tithes and offering. **Malachi 3: 8**

It is Amazing to see that the introduction of this verse opens up with a question. This is a question that everybody ought to consider carefully; *will a man be so daring to rob God?*

Who is man to dare rob God? Man, whose substance is not hidden from God. Man, who depends on God and derives his all from God. Man, whom God intricately put his being together. Will a man rob God, who is his source? This will actually be sore wickedness and ingratitude on the part of man to rob. But the word of the Lord said man robs God in ***tithes*** and ***offerings***.

The Bible says;

"Will a man rob or defraud God? Yet you rob and defraud Me. But you say, in what way do we rob or defraud You? [You have withheld your] tithes and offerings." Malachi 3: 8 (AMPC)

Remember that in Chapter two, we have seen a little of what tithes means. Now, let us consider something more profound about tithe.

God commands that all tithes should be brought into His store house. You might wonder why God requires all of our tithes; He knows that some persons may falter in this area.

More so, tithing is God's command and the inspiration behind tithing is obedience. It is a very simple and easy principle; please don't get me wrong, God's word never said that if you don't tithe, you are going to hell, No! What I am driving at is that your refusal to tithe will not take you to hell but you won't have the abundant life here on earth.

The main reason why we tithe is to obey God. We're simply obeying what His Word says and truthfully, it's just one or two things that we're going to do with the tithe. It is either we're going to **GIVE** it or we're going to **STEAL** it.

Additionally, you make a living by what you get. We make a lifestyle by what we give. When God is talking about giving, here is what he is trying to say to you; I'm trying to give something to you. I'm not trying to get something out of you. I'm trying to get something to you, so you can get everything I ever promised you and it's going to be perpetual and it is never going to stop; likewise, your harvest will be so huge like you've never seen before.

Your Harvest is greater than your seed

2 Corinthians 9:6 (AMPC)

[Remember] this: he who sows sparingly and grudgingly will also reap sparingly and grudgingly, and he who sows generously [that blessings may come to someone] will also reap generously and with blessings.

This might sound very ridiculous but it's the truth. Everything we have in our possession came from us giving. Not from us selling but from us sowing. We have sowed a lot of things, we have sowed cars. So, God has blessed us with many vehicles. We have sowed clothes so we don't get worried about anything that we put on. We have paid other people's rent so guess what? We don't ever pay or worry about ours because anything we got came from sowing.

I remember one time that we got ready to move into our new house. We sowed all my furniture and now in our new house, we got our new furniture and let me tell you what, it is fully paid for because what you sell that's the harvest but what you sow is up to God.

For instance, if I sell you something for $10, all I got is that $10. But if I sow the money as a seed and I put the price on what is sown. Evidently, you will never know what the harvest is going to be like.

In addition, everything I have today is a product of the seed that I had sown. I drive what I drive because I sowed to have it. I wear what I wear because I sowed to have it. I got this chair because I sowed everything we sit on. We gave away TVs, so we got brand-new TV.

Good measure, pressed down and shaken together

Luke 6:38 (AMPC)

Give, and [gifts] will be given to you; good measure, pressed down, shaken together, and running over, will they pour into [the pouch formed by] the bosom [of your robe and used as a bag]. For with the measure you deal out [with the measure you use when you confer benefits on others], it will be measured back to you.

See this; God will always outdo our giving and you can never out give God. Therefore, whenever something comes back with supernatural backing. It's always great. When God says go and give it to me and this is what I'm going to do for you. I'm going to give it back to you. Every time we exchange it. That's momentum. Give, give, give, give, give, give, that's momentum. Give, give, give, and give. Every time this exchange, you're going to come out with more than what you gave because this is what the Bible says good measure, pressed down and shaken together and running over.

Please let me explain this analogy, have you ever had some cornflakes? When You pour some of the cornflakes into a bowl and fill to the brim, obviously the bowl will no longer contain more but if you want to add more cornflakes into the bowl, you will see that it has to be crunched down before anymore could be added, well this trick is usually carried out by those that are on diet, especially when they are told that they could only take one bowl. That's how God wants us to practice giving. He says good measure, pressed down, shaken together.

Benefit of tithing

Malachi 3:11-12 (AMPC)

And I will rebuke the devourer [insects and plagues] for your sakes and he shall not destroy the fruits of your ground, neither shall your vine drop its fruit before the time in the field, says the Lord of hosts.

12 And all nations shall call you happy and blessed, for you shall be a land of delight, says the Lord of hosts.

Good news! God's promises are yes and Amen. He [God] will not say a thing and it will not come to pass.

Therefore, when God says 'He will,' He meant it. Coming to the benefits of tithing, God promised to prevent the devourer from taking what belongs to us. Devourers are like situation that takes away money from us unnecessarily, conditions of unfruitfulness, lack of progress in business and most especially financial challenges. Tithing keeps these types of situations far from us.

Tithing will make God step into any unruly situations in your life that want to steal your peace, joy, health, finances etc.

Now that you have learned about tithing don't you think it's high time to take a bold step of faith?

Try God with this.

Giving:

I was planning a vacation to Jamaica a few years ago. It was around the same time NBM purchased our new building. Instead of going to Jamaica all exclusive for five days I decided to sow a $1,000 seed into building renovation. I believed if I sowed into the renovation of NBM, God would renovate areas in my life. Fast forward to Feb., 2018, I started to believe God to purchase a home. I wrote the vision according to the word of God. I wrote the vision for my primary residence and also my desired vacation home (dream home). On 12/28/18, I signed the papers for my new home and moved in on 12/31/18. On 12/31/18, I turned the keys to my home that had everything I wrote not for my primary residence but I was turning the key to the home that had everything I had written for my vacation home (dream house). God far exceeds our greatest expectation. To God be the glory!

~ Pastor Adreane Russell

CHAPTER NINE

Right Attitude For Profitable Giving

Do you remember this popular saying that; *attitude is everything?*

Attitude truly is everything, as this eventually determines how far a person will go in life. Something unique about life is that, you cannot have a positive life with a negative mind.

Therefore, whenever you want to give, do it with a right attitude because God is more important than money.

Permit me to remind you a beautiful story of giving from the bible; the story of the widow's mite. In the story, Jesus gave a contrast between the widow and the rich men. The widow put in more than what others had, because she gave everything she has. But the rich men brought their lots out of the abundance that they had. It was seen that the woman's heart showed in her contribution.

Give with expectation of harvest

Having dealt with the attitude of giving, let me show you something more. It is one thing to give with a right attitude; it is another thing to expect a harvest of what we have sown.

Therefore, it's important that you know that the seeds that you sow, you got to have an expectation for them. You can't just throw them up in the air and let the wind take it whichever where it goes.

The Bible in Matthew 13:3 through 8 are clearly written in red. When they're in red, we know that Jesus is talking and whatever He says is very important and should be carefully adhered to.

Matthew 13:3-8 (AMPC)

3 And He told them many things in parables (stories by way of illustration and comparison), saying, A sower went out to sow.

4 And as he sowed, some seeds fell by the roadside, and the birds came and ate them up.

5 Other seeds fell on rocky ground, where they had not much soil; and at once they sprang up, because they had no depth of soil.

6 But when the sun rose, they were scorched, and because they had no root, they dried up and withered away.

7 Other seeds fell among thorns, and the thorns grew up and choked them out.

8 Other seeds fell on good soil, and yielded grain—some a hundred times as much as was sown, some sixty times as much, and some thirty.

Evidently, these verses reveal that the inspiration behind sowing a seed for offering is reward. Whenever you give, expect a reward for your giving. This implies that, in tithing, the reward is obedience. For seed sowing, offering is reward. So according to the above verses, it says that we can have a 30, 60 and a 100-fold blessing. It does not apply to your tithe. It does not apply to your first fruit. It does not apply to your alms. The 30,60 and a 100-fold blessing only applies to your offering which is also your seed which is also what you're going to sow.

Furthermore, the Apostle Paul said in the Bible that;

2 Corinthians 9:7 (AMPC)

The word 'Purpose in his heart' means that I [Paul] can't tell you what to give. Giving is a thing of the heart. Nobody should compel you to give.

Therefore, when you are asked to give, this should excite you. Givers who give from their heart enjoy the blessing that comes afterwards.

For example, when we say it's time to give, that should be the happiest time in church because that's the time to make an exchange rate. This means that I'm about to give to God and He is about to give me something great. Now, let our giving take a new turn. It's a season of abundance for you. Will you allow the little you have to keep you from the abundance that God wants you to enjoy?

Think about this. As a side note, it is also worthy to know that you can give in church whilst you are in church, not when watching the Apostle preaching from a television set. In front of the television, you are just being blessed alone, but you do not have the opportunity to also react to the word and give perhaps a 'thanks' offering to God whilst in church.

Luke 4:14-16 (KJV)

14 And Jesus returned in the power of the Spirit into Galilee: and there went out a fame of him through all the region round about. 15 And he taught in their synagogues, being glorified of all. 16 And he came to Nazareth, where he had been brought up: and, as his custom was, he went into the synagogue on the sabbath day, and stood up for to read.

"It was Jesus custom to go to church. So, I want to ask you, what makes you think you don't have to go to church? What make you think that you can worship and learn under some television preacher? You better stop letting the devil fool you and get established in a local church". ~ Bishop Bill McKinney

CHAPTER TEN

More Testimonials

1. A BLESSING

Apostle Gregory and Pastor Teresa McCurry & New Beginning Ministries have been a true blessing to ME and MY family from day one. May 9, 2010 Mother's Day was my first encounter with Apostle. My family and I were coming out of a domestic violence shelter that we had been in for 7 months. Life had been a real rollercoaster for myself and my family.

So, when given the invitation to visit New Beginning, I was somewhat skeptical. I had been hurt from So many things and church hurt was one. Stepping into that auditorium that morning i didn't what to expect. The woman that invited me promised me it wouldn't be normal church. That was so true. You could feel the love coming in. The Holy Spirit showed me love beyond measure.

God filled me up through Apostle Greg and his small congregation of what seemed like 15 people. God pointed me out to the apostle. he told me that God had me on his HEART that he knows my situation and that I was sent to New Beginning to get just that, a fresh start. God knew that MOVING into a new home from the shelter was a little overwhelming and that I needed a support system/team.

That's what the apostle became. Before the service was over the apostle and the congregation had a whole house full of furniture for my family. $900 to help with any extra experience that we may have had, and a car!! Look at God. God showed me that day to have faith, trust and believe he'll provide for me and my family. It was not a coincidence ending up in the Phyllis centre that morning. That was the beginning of our new beginning- Becoming the second member of New Beginning. To this day, I'm continuously being blessed. Thank YOU, Apostle Gregory, for all that YOU'VE done for me and my family.

~ Sis. Shanell Williams

***

2.

I was so Happy about being a tither and I was sharing with a friend how I encouraged another friend to start tithing, and she said to me, okay what did you say to that friend? With excitement, I said GOD wants you to tithe off your net and give an offering, and she said you told that person wrong. I said what? That's how you are supposed to tithe and she still said no.

Then she explained that you tithe off your gross, so I still don't get it. So, I prayed to GOD to reveal the truth to me. So, one morning I was listening to Creflo Dollar, and at the end of His message, he said for all you Christians talking about weather I tithe from my gross or from my net, he said Uncle Sam don't trust you, so you are going to give GOD the leftovers, and his message was over soon after. I wept like a baby and repented to GOD. GOD also requires the first fruit of all our increases.

~ **Sis. Shawnda Slaughter**

***

3.

I always thought that giving was never an issue for me. I would give clothes and other things that I was not using any longer to charities and the less fortunate. I didn't even mind giving a few dollars to people who needed it or giving of my time to help others. However, when I became a new Christian, I realized that giving my tithes was a struggle.

I started with only giving between $1.00 to $10.00; if I had a little extra money, I would give $20.00 but that was the maximum. I was in the mindset that I needed to keep the majority of my money to pay bills and God would not want me to be foolish and not have enough to survive. I was depending too much on my resources and not my source. As I grew in my faith, I began to Tithe from my net balance. That is after the government took their portion, my medical, dental and retirement got theirs and then I gave God his 10%.

I felt that I had really grown with my giving during that time and God began to move more on my behalf. At this time, I had become a single mother with a small child to take care of. Between food, clothes, day care and other essentials, there were times when I would have nothing left, but God provided. I never had anything cut off, we never were without food, and I still managed to pay at that time $520.00 per month for pre-school.

Although God was still keeping me afloat, I felt as if I needed more money in my pocket to feel complete. So, I began to get involved with the payday loan process. It was ok for a while until I had more than 1 at a time. I was borrowing from one loan place to pay back the other and it turned into a vicious cycle and it seemed like I would never get out.

I had to increase my Faith, renew my mind and know that God would supply all of my needs. I made the decision to pay all of the loans back and not ever borrow again and with the help of God, I have not been down that road in 12 years. There were times that I wanted to go back but one of my favourite scriptures, "seek ye first the kingdom of Heaven and all these things will be added unto you" (Matthew 6:33) kept me going.

God wanted me to stop relying on my own abilities and get closer to him, do more of his work, spend more time with him and everything that I desire can be mine. Romans 12:2 in the new living translation states that: "Don't copy the behaviour and customs of this world, but let God transform you into a new person by changing the way you think. Then you will learn to know God's will for you, which is good and pleasing and perfect" This scripture speaks to me because being a part of this world, we tend to want and do what we see others have and do. Only to realize that things are just things and once they get old, the desire fades. God has given me everything that I need to sustain. Once I came to this revelation, I realized that I should be tithing from my gross because without God's protection, grace and mercy, I would not be able to work and make money.

When he saw that he could trust me to be faithful and take care of his business, he began to stretch my harvest so much that I would have more left from my pay check than I ever had with the payday loans. Once I began tithing from my gross, bigger and better things began to happen because I trusted God's word and believed that he would not forsake me.

Today, I walk in Malachi 3:11, "God will rebuke the devourer for your sake" He makes a way for me on a daily basis, I do not worry about how anything will get done, I just rest in knowing that God is faithful. He made a way for me to go on my dream vacation to Paris in 2017 for little to nothing. When I filed bankruptcy and had to give up my car, he blessed me with a brand-new car a couple months later.

I could go on and on about his works, I am so grateful. He allows my resources to last until he blesses me with more. In addition to tithing, I am now becoming a person who can give offering and put a demand on what I give to return to me pressed down, shaken together and runneth over. I am thanking God to become even more of a sower. I know that his word is true.

~ Sis. Richanda Jackson

***

4. My Giving Testimony

In 2017 I was at a low, physically, and needed to be relieved from work for 6 months, in order to recover. Being the only source of income in my house I knew that I had to trust God to provide. (That was easy, I thought) and in the process I knew that I would have a pay decrease of 30%.

I stood under the teaching of Apostle Greg: Give back to God (cheerfully) what is His and have a love offering, and that's exactly what I did. I spoke with my wife that I will continue to give the same in tithe and offering, we will continue to trust the Almighty God and He will provide.

Because of God's love, my obedience and faith in God, that 6-month period, God provided for my house and there was no lack (Hallelujah) in my house. And 6months later I returned to work, not missing a beat.

~ Deacon Reginald Walker

QUESTIONS AND ANSWERS SECTION

Q. So do I tithe on everything?
A. Yes you tithe on all your increase, just bless God with your best

Q. Can I trust the church with my money?
A. No. You have to thrust God with your giving

Q. Is it okay to pause my tithing during tough financial times?
A. The Bible doesn't mention anything about "pausing" tithing. And it doesn't say we'll go to hell if we don't tithe. But get this: Many people have observed that after they stopped tithing, their finances seemed to get worse.

Q. Do I tithe on the gross or net of my pay check??
A. I tithe on my Gross, but I started with my net. It is your personal love affair with God!! Do you want a Net or Gross blessing??

GIVING

Q. What don't I tithe on?
A. All your increase

Q. What's the difference between tithing and offerings?
A. A tithe is an amount (a percentage of your income) and an offering is anything given beyond that, but not in place of the tithe.

Q. What If I sow a seed to a person and they buy liquor or drugs with the money??
A. That is a good question. Just remember that your duty is to fulfil the will of God, which is for you to give, once you do that, God is happy and that does not have anything to do with how the other person uses the money that you gave them

Q. Why does the church accept credit or debit cards?
A. Credit and Debit cards are a form of payment accepted by our country, you can also use those as a medium of giving your tithing in the House of God, what matters is that you are giving the amount that you are supposed to give to God and that it ends up in the account of the church.

ABOUT THE AUTHORS

Apostle Gregory McCurry

Apostle Gregory McCurry is the founder and senior pastor of New Beginning Ministries, a Cleveland-based church. He longs to see lives transformed by introducing;

"A Real God, To Real People With Real Issues."

He is ordained and faithfully submitted under the leadership of Apostle Leon D. Nelson Jr. of Embassy Ministries International. He has been preaching and teaching the good news of Jesus Christ for over twenty-five years. His motivating messages have reached many, transcending cultural and denominational barriers within the church and beyond.

Apostle Gregory McCurry offers counseling for men and couples. He has a passion to minister to men through a monthly men's meeting entitled "Men of Impact" in order to help them step up and be the men God has called them to be and serve the people of God.

He ministers with a knowledge born under biblically grounded principles together with a heavy prophetic anointing. When "hearing from heaven" under his prophetic mantle lives are changed, captives are set free, and the power of God is imparted as he is used mightily in the realm of the supernatural. This allows him to administer sage advice to both believers and non-believers.

With a home base in Olmsted Falls, Ohio, Apostle Greg is married to Pastor Teresa "Pastor T" McCurry. He has raised seven children and has a host of grandchildren.

Teresa (Pastor Tee) McCurry

Pastor Teresa McCurry is an ordained minister of the Gospel of Jesus Christ; she co-labours with her husband, Apostle Gregory McCurry, of New Beginning Ministries, doing the work of the Lord as a ministry team.

"We introduce a Real God, to Real people with Real issues"

Pastor Tee was called to ministry in 2010 under the leadership of Apostle Leon and Pastor Margie Nelson. She has travelled extensively, educating and inspiring others with her unique approach of conveying information. She has a heart for doing missions work around the world.

This was the beginnings of a great and powerful deliverance move of God in her life to reach the lost and hurting. God anointed Pastor Tee with a spiritual eye sight and ability to speak into people's lives and immediately a deliverance takes place to bring forth healing to broken hearted souls and to proclaim liberty to the captives and set their hearts completely free.

Pastor Tee is dedicated to helping people who seek to make a positive change.

Her marketplace ministry extends beyond the walls of the church. She is a Beauty Entrepreneur Coach, International Keynote Speaker/Bible Teacher & Church Leadership Trainer, Author of the book Runnin' Things; The Resilient spirit of an Entrepreneur, a licensed cosmetologist with over 30 years of beauty industry experience. She has a Bachelor's degree in Applied Business Administration.

She is currently the President & CIO of Inspire Me Incorporated, Salon Manager at The Salon at ULTA Beauty and, she Co- chairs Christian Networking Entrepreneurs "CNE". We encourage creative thinking, inspire meaningful dialogue & Promote Personal & Business development, through fellowship that will spotlight and support Christian businesses.

She is the founder of The MCS Fund, whose sole mission is to generate unrestricted funds for Sickle Cell Anemia affected individuals. Through Supportive

Services & Advocacy serving the needs of people plagued by this disease is not only a mission, but a passion.

Apostle and Pastor McCurry are both available for speaking engagement, workshops & seminars at:

Email: Info@mynewbeginning.org
Phone: (216) 916-9270 ext. 4
Website: www.MyNewBeginning.org,
2060 West 65th Street Cleveland, Ohio 44102

Appendix 1: Resources Used

https://www.investopedia.com
https://www.blueletterbible.org
https://www.biblegateway.com
https://www.gotquestions.org/
https://www.youtube.com/watch?v=UWAXyDUjfv8&t=118s

LeTonya F. Moore, JD is an attorney-entrepreneur with almost twenty years of experience building and helping build successful enterprises. She is the visionary behind 360° Brand Protection Strategies™, developed to address the holistic needs of the entrepreneur. The 360° methodology enables brands to develop strategic growth and expansion to the national, international, and global marketplace. Recently, LeTonya reached a major milestone of introducing her brand protection methodology to the United Kingdom in 2018. She is the founding member of The Global Growth Group (G3), a society of experts collaborating to provide entrepreneurs, including speakers, authors, and coaches with a guided pathway to global protecting their brand both in the US and abroad. Through her work, she is now affectionately known as the Global Brand Protector ™

LeTonya is a sought after speaker who brings value and shares priceless insight and wisdom with her audiences. LeTonya is no stranger to overcoming obstacles and living life on purpose, with purpose. She shares her success story in her, "LeTonya Speaks" motivational presentations that spread a message of faith, perseverance, and the hard work to audiences small and large. LeTonya's "Real Talk" presentation style proves enlightening, educational, and entertaining for diverse demographics.

SPEAKING TOPICS
1. BRAND PROTECTION: LOOKING BEYOND PATENTS, TRADEMARKS, & COPYRIGHTS
2. BUILDING A B.A.I.L. TEAM: PROTECTING YOUR $, YOUR BOOKS, YOUR ASSETS, & YOUR LEGACY
3. 6 M's of BRAND PROTECTION: MINDEST, MOTIVATION, MONIKER, MONEY, MARKETING, & MASTERY
4. HOW TO STOP BRAND STEALING THIEVES WITH A BRAND PROTECTION PLAYBOOK
5. THE TRAILBLAZEHER ™: MY JOURNEY FROM TEEN MOM TO GLOBAL BRAND PROTECTOR

To learn more about LeTonya Moore visit her official website at www.letonyamoore.com.
Follow her on Facebook @iprotectyourbrand
Follow her on Twitter/IG/Snapchat/LinkedIn @letonyamoore
Direct Dial: 256-472-2631 Schedule Consult

GIVING

GREGORY & TERESA MCCURRY

GIVING

The Agent-Owned Cloud Brokerage®

Let Pamela help you make your realty dreams a reality!

*Buying   *Selling   *First-Time Buyer   *Investor   *Relocation   *Career

Pamela is a licensed REALTOR® in the Commonwealth of Virginia

Not in Virginia? No Problem

We're in all fifty states; I can connect you with an agent who services your area.   Call me , visit my website, or like me on Face Book.

Interested in a career in real estate? To explore a career with Exp Realty
Go to:

http://pamelawestbrook.exprealty.careers/

Pamela Westbrook

Broker/**REALTOR®**

(866) 825-7169 Ext. 456

Email: Pamela.westbrook@exprealty.com

Website: pamelawestbrook.exprealty.com

Facebook—www.facebook.com/pwestbrookrealestate

www.ingramcontent.com/pod-product-compliance
Lightning Source LLC
Chambersburg PA
CBHW020943090426
42736CB00010B/1244